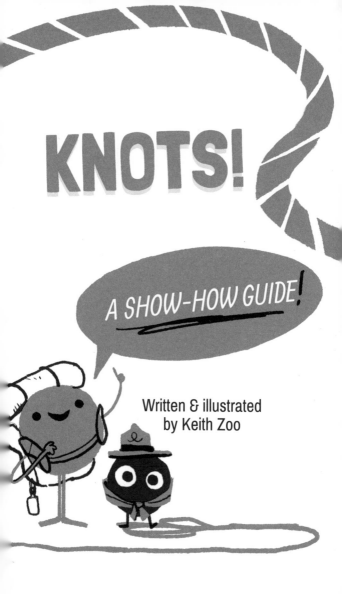

KNOTS!

A SHOW-HOW GUIDE!

Written & illustrated
by Keith Zoo

ODD DOT • NEW YORK

Hey there!

This **Show-How** gives you the know-how on knots. We've included only the essentials so you can easily master the FUN-damentals. You'll be bending, binding, and looping in no time. Ready? Let's go!

MATERIALS NEEDED:

ROPE OR STRING

SCISSORS

TYPES OF KNOTS IN THIS BOOK

Hitch Knot:
Ties a rope to an object

Bend Knot:
Ties two ropes together

Bind Knot:
Ties two objects together

Stopper Knot:
Prevents a rope from passing through a hole

Loop Knot:
Forms a fixed loop in a rope

TABLE OF CONTENTS

TIP:
Don't worry if your first attempts aren't perfect. Try again and keep practicing; soon you'll master all the knots in this book!

HITCH KNOTS
LARK'S HEAD

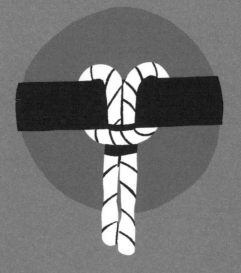

Possible Use: Tie a string to a ring to make a necklace.

1

WORKING ENDS

STANDING END →

2

3

4 Pull down working ends to tighten knot!

HITCH KNOTS
CLOVE HITCH

Possible Use: Tie a rope to two trees and throw a tarp over it for a quick tent.

NDING
END

WORKING
END

2

4

Pull working
end up
through
center

Hold standing
end in place

3

DOUBLE HALF HITCH

Possible Use: Tie to a deck post to help secure a boat from sailing away.

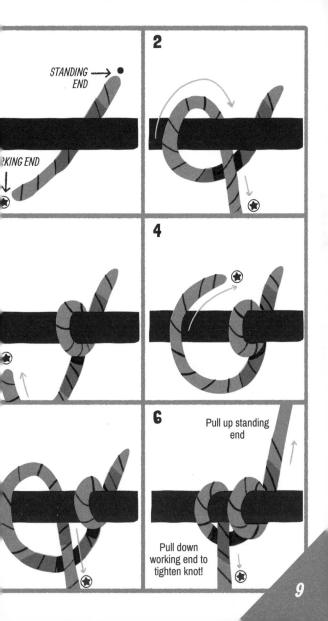

2

STANDING END

WORKING END

4

6

Pull up standing end

Pull down working end to tighten knot!

4

TAUTLINE HITCH

Possible Use: Tie to attach cargo onto a vehicle. This knot is also used to climb trees.

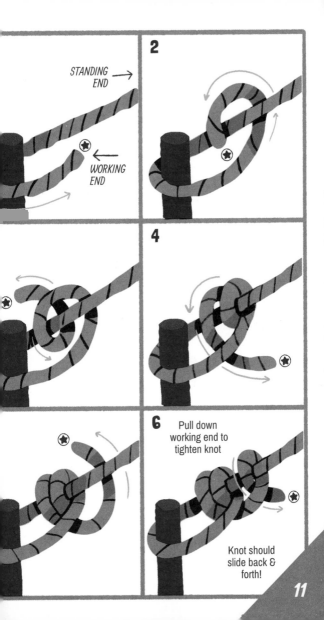

STANDING END →

← **WORKING END**

2

4

6 Pull down working end to tighten knot

Knot should slide back & forth!

11

5

BEND KNOTS
SQUARE KNOT
OR "REEF KNOT"

Possible Use: Tie two colors of embroidery floss together when making bracelets.

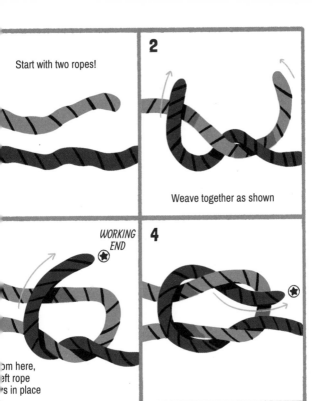

2

Start with two ropes!

Weave together as shown

WORKING END ✪

om here,
eft rope
s in place

4

✪

Pull both sides away from
the other to tighten knot!

6

BEND KNOTS
SHEET BEND

Possible Use: Sailors use this knot to tie ropes to their sails!

WORKING END ⊛

Start with two ropes!

STANDING END ●

2

⊛

⊛

Pull all four loose ends to tighten knot!

MAKING KNOTS CAN BE REALLY TOUGH!

DON'T GIVE UP!

BEND KNOTS
BUTTERFLY

Possible Use: Rock climbers use
this knot in a pinch to isolate
a worn section of rope!

WORKING ENDS

Loop two pieces of rope together as shown

2

ntly pull down
rking ends to
ighten knot

TIP!

Hold the knot with your fingers while you tighten it to help keep it in place!

8

BEND KNOTS
NAIL KNOT

★ BEFORE YOU START ★
You'll need a small hollow tube that's wider than your string.

Possible Use: Tie together two lines of a fishing hook to fly-fish.

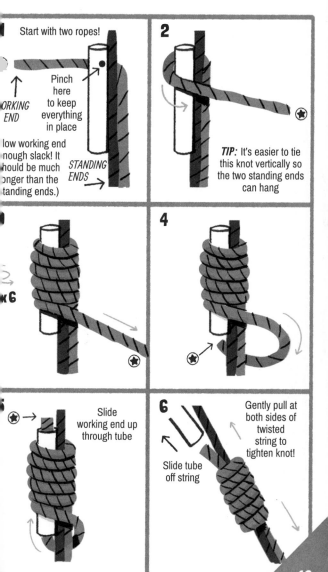

Start with two ropes!

↑
ORKING
END

Pinch here to keep everything in place

low working end nough slack! It hould be much onger than the tanding ends.)

STANDING ENDS →

2

✶

TIP: It's easier to tie this knot vertically so the two standing ends can hang

×6

✶

4

✶

✶ →

Slide working end up through tube

6

Gently pull at both sides of twisted string to tighten knot!

Slide tube off string

9

DOUBLE FISHERMAN'S KNOT

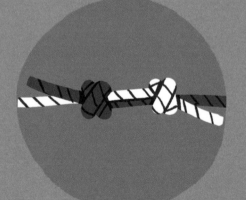

Possible Use: Rock climbers use this knot if they need to join two ropes!

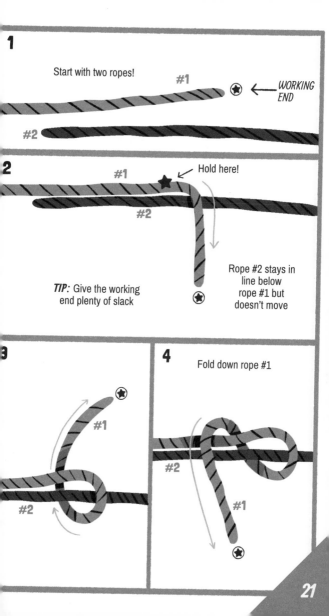

1

Start with two ropes!

#1

WORKING END

#2

2

#1

Hold here!

#2

Rope #2 stays in line below rope #1 but doesn't move

TIP: Give the working end plenty of slack

3

#1

#2

4

Fold down rope #1

#2

#1

21

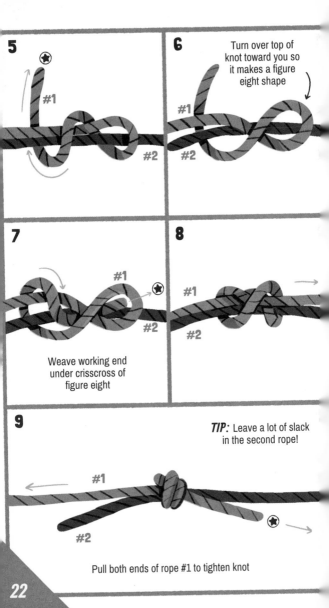

5

#1

6

Turn over top of knot toward you so it makes a figure eight shape

#1

#2

#2

7

#1

#2

Weave working end under crisscross of figure eight

8

#1

#2

9

TIP: Leave a lot of slack in the second rope!

#1

#2

Pull both ends of rope #1 to tighten knot

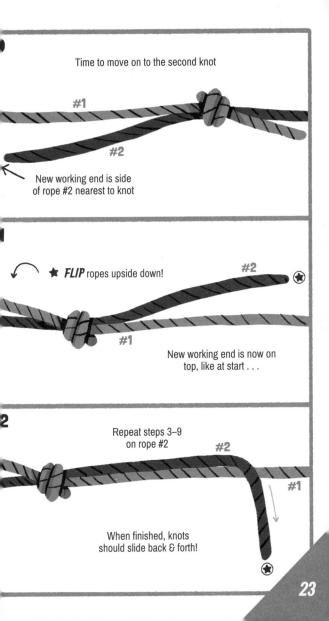

Time to move on to the second knot

#1

#2

New working end is side
of rope #2 nearest to knot

★ **FLIP** ropes upside down!

#2 ✪

#1

New working end is now on
top, like at start . . .

Repeat steps 3–9
on rope #2

#2

#1

When finished, knots
should slide back & forth!

✪

23

10

BIND KNOTS

BOA CONSTRICTOR

Possible Use: Tie together a bunch of new pencils and give them as a gift to a friend.

Loop rope twice & pull taut at both ends

STANDING END

WORKING END

2

Hold standing end in place & twist working end to left to make figure eight

Weave object through both loops

4

Pull both sides taut to tighten!

11

MILLER'S KNOT

Possible Use: Millers once used this knot to tie up large sacks of grains!

Arrange rope as shown

2

Weave working end
underneath crisscross

Pull both ends taut to tighten knot!

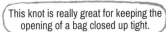

This knot is really great for keeping the
opening of a bag closed up tight.

27

BIND KNOTS
BUTCHER'S KNOT

Possible Use: Tie to secure boxes
and tie up food for cooking.

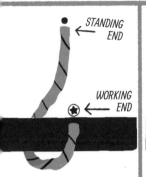

STANDING END

WORKING END

2

4 Pull taut

5 Switch working ends

Hold up standing end

anding is now your orking end

7 Pull taut & cut off loose ends!

13

STOPPER KNOTS
FIGURE EIGHT

Possible Use: Tie to stop other knots from coming apart!

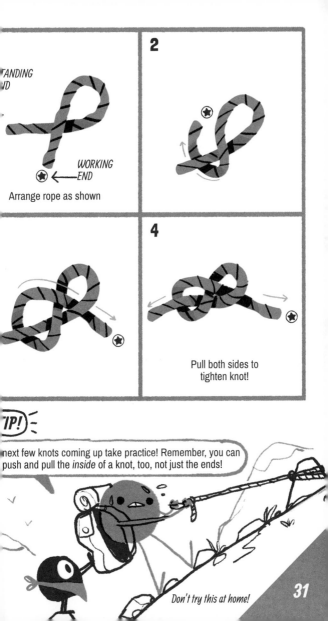

*TANDING
~~D~~

**WORKING
END**

Arrange rope as shown

2

4

Pull both sides to
tighten knot!

TIP!

next few knots coming up take practice! Remember, you can
push and pull the *inside* of a knot, too, not just the ends!

Don't try this at home!

14

BUTTON
KNOT

Possible Use: Tie in place of
a button on a sweater.

Arrange rope as shown

Leave slack for working end!

WORKING END ⟶ ✴

STANDING END ⟵ •

2

over / under / over / under

4 Adjust loops as shown

Working end should still have some ✴ slack

over / under / over

6 Gently pull both ends & work inner loops to tighten!

TIP: This knot takes a little bit of patience & practice.

15

STOPPER KNOTS

FRIENDSHIP KNOT

Possible Use: Tie around your wrist and cut the loose ends off to make a bracelet.

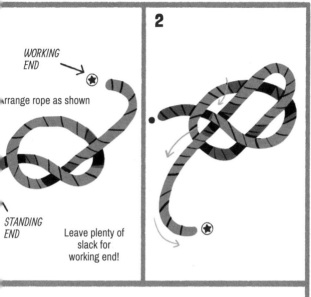

WORKING END

arrange rope as shown

STANDING END

Leave plenty of slack for working end!

2

Weave working end back through—under / over / under / over

Gently pull both working & standing ends. Work inner loops to tighten

TIP: This knot works best with a stiff rope & may take a little practice!

16

STOPPER KNOTS
MONKEY FIST

Possible Use: Tie the two loose ends to a key ring to make a key chain.

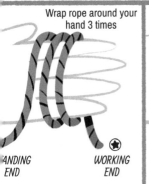

Wrap rope around your
hand 3 times

*STANDING
END*

*WORKING
END*

2

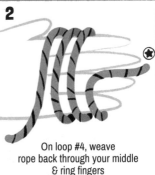

On loop #4, weave
rope back through your middle
& ring fingers

Slide your hand out & hold
loops in place

Wrap working end up
around like this

4

x3

Tighten just enough to be
able to hold loops in place

Thread working end
through top loops

& then thread it back
through bottom loops

6

Wrap working end
around center loops

Gently pull both ends &
work inner loops
to tighten

37

THIS KNOT TAKES A LITTLE PATIENCE!

17

LOOP KNOTS
OVERHAND

Possible Use: Tie at the end of a kite string to keep the string on your finger while your kite is in the air.

Arrange rope as shown

WORKING
END

STANDING
END

Pull both sides taut to tighten knot!

18

LOOP KNOTS
NONSLIP LOOP

Possible Use: Tie to your fishing lure.

Weave rope as shown

STANDING END

Give plenty of slack to both ends!

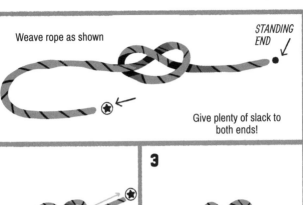

3

x3

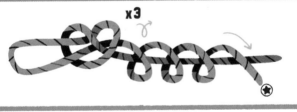

Pull both ends taut to tighten!

19

LOOP KNOTS
PERFECTION LOOP

Possible Use: Tie to your boat anchor
before you drop it in the water.

WORKING
END
↓
⊛

NDING
→ ●

rrange rope as shown. Give lots
of slack to working end!

2

⊛

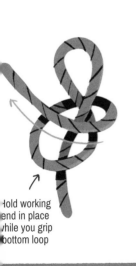

Hold working
end in place
while you grip
bottom loop

4

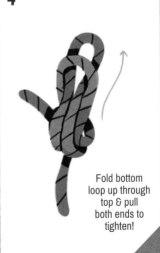

Fold bottom
loop up through
top & pull
both ends to
tighten!

43

20

LOOP KNOTS
BOWLINE

Possible Use: Use this knot to rescue someone who fell down a hole!

Arrange rope as shown

STANDING END

WORKING END

2

Pull loop & working end down to tighten knot!

Pssst . . . Hey, we said *bowline* knot. Not *bow tie*.

KNOT USES

Knots can be used to do all sorts of tasks.
Here are a few more real-world examples:

A. Secure your tent lines using a **tautline hitch**.
B. Bundle some sticks together with a **boa constrictor knot**.
C. A **nail knot** would be great for attaching a lure to a fishing line.
D. Keep your scarf or bandana around your neck using an **overhand loo**
E. Attach a rope to a post using a **clove hitch**.

An imprint of Macmillan Publishing Group, LLC
120 Broadway, New York, NY 10271
OddDot.com

Text and illustrations copyright © 2020 by Keith Zoo

Library of Congress Cataloging-in-Publication Data is available.
ISBN 978-1-250-24995-1

Editor: Justin Krasner
Cover designer: Tim Hall & Colleen AF Venable
Interior designer: Colleen AF Venable

Our books may be purchased in bulk for promotional,
educational, or business use. Please contact your local bookseller
or the Macmillan Corporate and Premium Sales Department at
(800) 221-7945 ext. 5442 or by email at
MacmillanSpecialMarkets@macmillan.com.

Show-How Guides is a trademark of Odd Dot.
Printed in China by Hung Hing Off-set Printing Co. Ltd., Heshan City,
Guangdong Province
First edition, 2020

10 9 8 7 6 5 4 3 2 1

22G3121

Keith Zoo

is an artist and illustrator
living in Massachusetts. You
can find more of his work
at keithzoo.com and on
Instagram @keithzoo.

DATE